New in New Zealand

W0046664

Kate Absolum

New in
New Zealand

DELTA Publishing

You can listen to *New in New Zealand* using the free DELTA Augmented app – you'll also find fun interactive activities!

Download the free DELTA Augmented app onto your device	Start picture recognition and scan the **contents page**	Download files and use them now or save them for later

Apple and the Apple logo are trademarks of Apple Inc., registered in the US and other countries. App Store is a service mark of Apple Inc. | Google Play and the Google Play logo are trademarks of Google Inc.

1st edition   1 ⁵⁴³²¹ | 2026 25 24 23 22

Delta Publishing, 2022
www.deltapublishing.co.uk

© Ernst Klett Sprachen GmbH, Rotebühlstraße 77, 70178 Stuttgart, 2022

Author: Kate Absolum
Editor: Kate Baade
Annotations and activities: Megan Roderick

Cover and layout: Andreas Drabarek, Eva Lettenmayer
Illustrations: Anna Knopf, Beehive Illustration
Design: Datagroup int, Timisoara
Cover picture: Anna Knopf, Beehive Illustration
Printing and binding: Salzland Druck, Staßfurt

ISBN 978-3-12-501156-4

Contents

Abbreviations

sb   somebody
sth   something

Before you start

1. If you had to move with your family to another country to live, how would you feel? Write words in your own language and English.

my feelings	
My first language	English

2. Identify the feelings in your list as positive or negative. Tick the positive words and cross the negative ones.

3. What do you know about the country of New Zealand? Find out and write down five facts.

Facts about New Zealand

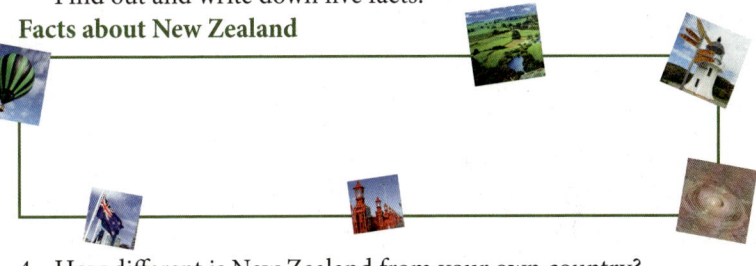

4. How different is New Zealand from your own country? Write a list of points.

5. Is being different good or bad? Read the story and find out how Maggie coped with a different way of life.

Chapter 1

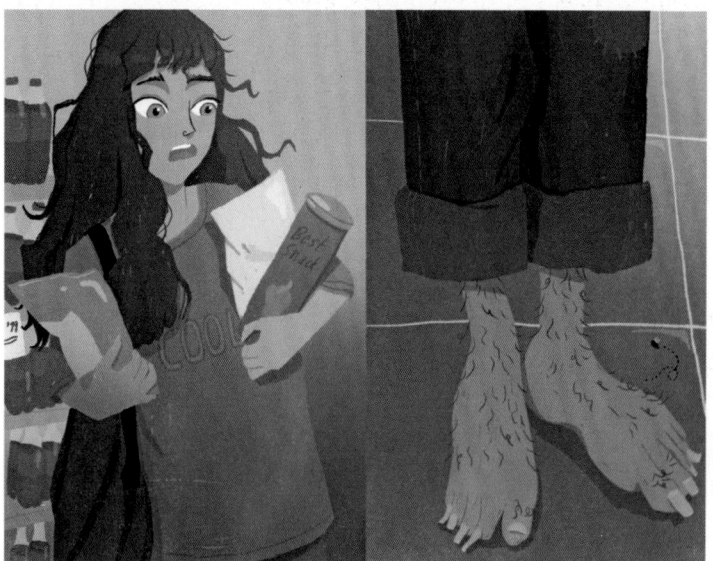

It was the bare feet in the supermarket that did it.

They were ugly feet too. Hairy toes, with long toenails that needed cutting. I really didn't get it. Why would you go barefoot to the supermarket? It's freezing cold and wet out there. It's the middle of July.

I know, I know, that sounds weird – freezing cold in the middle of July? Surely that's summer, right? Don't worry, this isn't some dystopian novel set in the future where shoes have disappeared and it rains all the time, although, to be honest it sometimes feels like it.

No, it's somewhere else entirely.

But I guess I need to rewind right?

Who am I? Where am I? ... And why am I talking so much about *feet*?

---

25 **dystopian** an imagined way of life that is difficult and frightening – 29 **to rewind** to go back to the beginning

Right. Well, the first question is easy. My name is Maggie and I'm 15 years old. I'm from London. That's London in England, England – as in the United Kingdom. You know, the place with the Queen, the Beatles, tea, castles. Normally, we live in London, where I'm a normal girl who goes to normal school with all her normal, shoe-wearing friends. I was having a lovely normal life, hanging out at the shops, meeting cute boys, going out with my friends at the weekend. Sweet, normal, usual.

But then my mum did something stupid. Really stupid.

I wasn't expecting it because she's normally smart, my mum. She's a doctor, but she specialises in the menopause. I know what you are thinking, gross, right? Yes. It basically means she wants to talk about hormones and periods all the time. God, going through puberty was a nightmare. She wanted to discuss it with me ALL the TIME.

It's just me and my mum and my baby brother, Stevie. Well, he isn't so much of a baby now; he is an annoying eight-year-old. He has cute little ringlets and a dimple on the side of one cheek, and he looks a bit like one of those baby angels, which is ironic because he is more like a demon. But I'm getting ahead of myself again.

It was a normal Tuesday night. I'd finished high school for the day and then picked up Stevie from school. The rule is we must get out of our school uniforms, do our music practice, and I must make afternoon tea. Then we can do whatever until Mum gets home (except bake, because I once set fire to the oven when Mum was out).

So yes, it was just a normal day, Stevie and I were on our computers when my mum, Louise, came home. She looked just as usual; a bit tired – but there was a weird vibe coming off her. She put down her bags, and said, "I'm calling a family meeting."

---

11 **menopause** the time when a woman stops menstruating (around 50) – 14 **puberty** the time of physical change between childhood and adulthood – 18 **ringlets** curls – 18 **dimple** a small hollow place on your cheeks when you smile

We both looked up from our screens - expecting her to say something like, we are all going to join in with meat-free Monday (the last time she called a family meeting she did this).

Instead, she said, "I've been offered a new job."

And we were both like, "OK, Mum that's great, yes! Well done etc, When does it start etc?" trying to sound like we were supportive, but I know we both wanted to get back to our screens.

"I start at the end of June. It's a really good <u>opportunity</u> – lots more money and a real opportunity to make a difference and … it's in New Zealand."

My mouth dropped open. I felt cold all over. Stevie was so shocked he dropped his tablet.

I don't often swear, but I did let out a big, "WHAT THE ****?

"I know it's not ideal, but it's a really decent job and they've offered me a contract for two years. So, I thought we should give it a go," she said in a rush.

Stevie's face went red. "I don't want to go to New Zealand."

He started to cry, "I don't even know where it is."

I said, "I don't want to go either. I'm happy here!"

Mum looked stressed. She's quite an attractive woman, I think. She has dark brown curly hair, but unlike mine, hers sits nicely and doesn't look like a haystack on her head. She has blue eyes - that often look a bit tired - and black glasses. She does have an unfortunate habit of wearing those bad clothes that women past forty like. I don't know why? It makes them look like their bodies are out of balance, with one hem lower than the other.

I looked at my brother, I don't usually agree with him but really, moving us to New Zealand in a month's time is a terrible idea.

Mum said, "It's a fantastic opportunity and I think we should go." She started listing all the reasons.

---

7 **supportive** helpful and encouraging – 13 **to swear** to use offensive language –
22 **haystack** a large pile of hay in the fields – 26 **hem** the bottom part of trousers, a dress, etc

"No," I said sharply, "I'm not going, and you can't make me." I stood up, closed my laptop, and stomped off, slamming the door for good measure.

…….. Well, famous last words, right?

Through a mixture of guilt (my career, I'm lonely, think about all the opportunities you might have, your brother is on his screen too much and he needs more of an outdoor life and so do you), threats (knife crime and teenagers in London), and bribery (the newest tablet for Stevie, and notebook for me) Mum managed to get us out of the country, our house rented, and to a new country in a little under a month.

So, even though I thought we were fine and happy as we were, we are moving to New Zealand.

And I don't even know where it is.

> What words does Maggie use to describe typical English life?

> What does Maggie mean when she says 'Famous last words …'?

Think about it…

> Why is it difficult for parents and children to agree sometimes?

> Are teenage years more difficult in that respect? How? Why?

---

2 **to stomp off** to walk away angrily – 2 **to slam** to close (a door) loudly – 8 **threat** when sb talks about bad things that might happen to you – 9 **bribery** persuading sb to do sth by offering rewards

Chapter 2

"Wake up Maggie."

Someone is rubbing my arm, and although I am really hoping it is Harry Styles, when I open my eyes, I see it's just Mum, reaching across the seats of the airplane.

"Mum, I *just* got to sleep, why are you waking me up?"

My mouth feels dry. I rub my eyes.

"You've been asleep for a while," she says, "and we are about to land so I thought you might like to look out the window."

"I'd rather still be asleep."

She frowned at me. Stevie was still asleep between us, his head hanging at a weird angle.

This plane ride to New Zealand was the worst. I have flown quite a lot in the past. We used to visit my grandparents in France every summer. Sometimes my mum would leave us there and come back and work. The last couple of times we've even flown back by ourselves, because I'm old enough to look after Stevie, if he is reasonable and not in his full-on 'demon-child' mode.

(You are probably wondering why it's just me, my brother, and
my mum. What happened to my dad? Well, I never had a dad.
We had another mum – Joanna, but she died of cancer when I
was seven and Stevie was just a baby. I don't remember her much.
Just that she had red hair and smelt like honey, and she used to   5
make my other mum laugh.)

But this plane ride to New Zealand was different to all those
flights.

Don't tell anyone, but I actually had been looking forward to it.
I like being able to watch unlimited movies and people bringing   10
me food. Aside from the fact that you can't use your phone. I
mean what's with that anyway. People can go to the moon, but I
can't text my friends from a plane ride? Now, *that's* stupid.

Anyway, Mum had sent on a bunch of our stuff, so we just had
a suitcase each. The plane was stylish inside, all black leather,   15
but the air stewards were wearing weird, patterned clothes that
looked like someone had thrown up on them. Mum let me have
the aisle seat. I put my headphones on and looked at the movies.
We were going to fly to Dubai, change planes, fly to Melbourne,
and then fly on to New Zealand from there. When I clicked on   20
the flight display, I realised it was seven hours just to Dubai. My
heart sank.

The seats were small. Stevie, of course, was happy playing
his video games, tongue slightly stuck out. Mum had had her
computer open for most of it, working, and she looked tired.   25

I felt bad. I guess I haven't been the easiest person to be around.
I mean I hadn't thrown any major tantrums, well, not after my
first big one anyway. I just don't really want to move to New
Zealand. But Mum has made me promise to try. If I tried, she said
she would buy me the latest notebook I wanted for Christmas.   30

---

10 **unlimited** a very large number or amount – 17 **to throw up** to be physically sick –
18 **aisle seat** the seat next to the passage between rows of seats – 27 **tantrum**
unreasonable or bad behaviour

Anyway, I was awake now, so I looked out the window. The sky was big and blue. There were white clouds.

"The Māori name for NZ is Aotearoa," Mum said. "That can be translated as 'the land of the long white cloud.'"

Great, I thought. We are moving to a small country in the Pacific that's named after a cloud. So much for getting tanned and wearing a bikini in a South Pacific Paradise, it's obviously just going to rain.

…

Outside the airport, we got a taxi. It was raining and everything looked green and wet. There was a lot of grass and trees. All the houses were single story and detached. They looked like toy houses. I felt nervous. To make myself feel better I started poking Stevie.

---

31 **to poke** *(here)* to push your finger into sb's side or arm

"Stop it, Maggie," he said, "Mum!"

I whisked my hand away. "What? I'm not doing anything."

I looked innocent. Then I poked him again.

"Mum!" he shouted.

Mum rubbed her forehead.

"Maggie, would you just stop that? We are all tired and you are making it worse. Again. Come on. You promised."

We stopped in front of our house and got out of the taxi. It looked very different from our terrace house in London. Mum looked around. She said, "Oh dear, this wasn't quite what I expected."

There was just so much grass around it. The house was made of wood. It had a big bay window overlooking the street and three steps leading up to a small deck at the front. The street looked ok, there were trees up and down it and a primary school that Stevie would go to. I'd get the school bus from around the corner.

Mum paid the taxi driver, and we lugged our suitcases up the stairs.

Mum opened the door. The walls were painted beige and the floors were wooden. It was cold and empty, nothing like our little cosy home in London. It was pre-furnished, and all the furniture looked like it was purchased for how hard-wearing it would be. In the living room the sofa was brown and had a sticky fake leather feel.

Mum frowned again.

"A few bright cushions and rugs, it will look much more homely," she said hopefully.

I wheeled my suitcase to my room. It was also cold. The walls were beige and the duvet had toothpaste-coloured stripes on it. SO ugly. I started composing a message to my friends in London describing the hell hole.

Stevie called from his room, "Muuuuum, I'm hungry!"

---

2 **to whisk away** to move sth rapidly out of sight – 17 **to lug** to carry or drag sth heavy – 23 **fake** not genuine or real – 30 **to compose** to write (letters, music)

Mum gave herself a shake, "Yes of course, I'd forgotten its breakfast time."

She opened a few of the cupboards in the kitchen.

"Oh dear, there isn't any food."

5 Stevie wailed. You have to be careful if you get between Stevie and food when he is hungry.

"Ok, ok. Let's go out and get something to eat."

"I don't want to," I said. "I'm tired and I look terrible."

"But I'm *hungry*, Maggie," Stevie shouted at me. His face going 10 red.

"Maggie, come on," Mum said, "I don't want to leave you here alone. You don't have anyone to call if there is a problem."

I frowned. Honestly, I just wanted to sleep, but also, I really didn't want to be in the house alone, who knew if there was a 15 Kiwi serial killer just waiting to pounce on me? I begrudgingly squashed a hat over my frizzy hair and stomped out of the house.

It was grey, and cold outside. So much for a sunny pacific paradise. The streets were wide. It was ten o'clock in the morning here, but who knows when the last time I slept was. I had no idea 20 what time it was in London.

A jogger ran past us. He didn't look at us weirdly, so that was good. There was a large green steep hill looming over us. We walked up to the bottom of it. On it was a sign: 'Maungawhau, Mt Eden.'

25 Mum said, "This is Mt Eden. It's a volcano. Actually, Auckland is built on something like sixty volcanoes."

"What? I can't believe you bought us to place that is *literally* built on volcanoes. Aren't they dangerous?"

Stevie was looking around like he wanted to crawl and hide 30 under car.

---

5 **wail** *(here)* to complain loudly – 13 **to frown** to make an angry expression by moving your eyebrows together – 15 **to pounce on sb** to attack sb – 15 **begrudgingly** without really wanting to – 16 **to squash** *(here)* to press sth down roughly – 16 **frizzy** hair that is curly and difficult to control

"No, don't worry. They are all dormant or extinct, or …
something. I can't remember which one, but they aren't
dangerous. Let's walk up and I'll show you."

Stevie and I groaned.

"Come on," she said sharply, "this will be good for your jet lag." 5

We slowly walked up the winding road. There were a lot of
people also walking and biking up the hill. I guess Aucklanders
are fit. I don't think I'd ever seen so many people in active wear
doing exercise. Usually in London, people just wore the stretchy
clothes to the café, but they didn't do any real exercise. 10

The road up Mt Eden was steep. After the first bend it was
closed to cars. The trees all looked different to the ones in
London. Even the birds were making different noises. There was
also a hum of something else in the air that I didn't recognise.
Insect noises of some kind, I think. 15

"Wow," said Stevie. The city was in front of us.

On the left-hand side was a deep crater covered in green grass.
In front of us apartment blocks and commercial buildings were
clustered together around a taller tower. Behind these was the
bridge, reaching across a blue harbour. 20

"That's the Harbour Bridge and the North Shore," said Mum.

To the right of the Harbour Bridge was another mountain that
looked like a volcano too. Mum looked at her phone.

"That's Rangitoto," she said trying to pronounce it correctly.
"It's the biggest volcano in Auckland. Isn't this a beautiful city? 25
I'm so glad we decided to give it a try."

It started raining again. I could feel my hair frizzing up under
my hat.

"Not *that* special," I said.

30

---

1 **dormant** volcano: not currently active but could still become active in the future –
1 **extinct** volcano: permanently inactive – 4 **to groan** to make a complaining noise – 5 **jet
lag** the tired feeling you get after long-distance flights – 17 **crater** of a volcano: the round
open part – 19 **to cluster together** to be together in a tight group

Mum rolled her eyes at me, "Come on, Maggie. We are in a city at the bottom of the world that has volcanos in it! I mean how cool is that?"

"More like dangerous," I muttered under my breath.

"Yes well, it's less dangerous than teenage knife crime in London," she snapped back.

We turned down the hill and walked down a long road, with stone walls on each side. We kept walking in silence. The air smelled green and earthy. Two men dressed in Lycra cycled in formation past us, hunched over their slimline bicycles, not very slimline themselves.

"Come on," said Mum, looking at her phone. "There's a supermarket near here. Let's go get some things to eat and then we'll go home."

I sighed. More walking. The supermarket when we finally got there was weird, all the food looked different. The bright lights made my head hurt. It started raining even more heavily outside. I could hear the rain thundering on the roof of the supermarket.

A man pushed by me to get to the counter.

"You are standing in the wrong place," he said.

"Go stand over there," he pointed out the end of the long queue to us.

Stevie was tugging on Mum's hand whinging about not being allowed to buy chocolate. I was tired, cold, hungry and miles from all my friends and I just knew my hair was doing its best impression of a haystack. Then I looked down and saw the bare feet of the person in front of me in the queue. They were ugly feet too. Hairy toes, with long toenails, which needed cutting. I really didn't get it. Why would you go bare foot to the supermarket?

---

4 **to mutter** to speak in a low voice, in a complaining way – 10 **slimline** of a bike: designed to have the least resistance when riding fast – 23 **to whinge** to complain in a childish way – 25 **to do an impression of** to look or sound like sb/sth else

It's freezing cold and wet out there. It's the middle of July. And it's unhygienic to wear bare feet to the supermarket, surely? Not to mention dangerous.

"That's just disgusting!" I whispered at Mum. I knew I was going to hate it here.

She sighed, "Well *maybe* people do things differently here, Maggie. Look, can you just try not to be so negative all of the time?"

In what ways were Maggie's first impressions of New Zealand different from a 'sunny, pacific paradise'?

What struck Maggie about the people they saw as they were walking?

Think about it...

Why was Maggie being negative about their arrival in NZ?

Who do you feel more sorry for – Maggie or Maggie's mother? Why?

2 **unhygienic** not clean or good for your health

Chapter 3

After a week in this stupid new city, where it rained every day, it was time to start school.

Mum woke me up with French toast in bed. She bought me in a plate and helped me sit up.

"Do I really have to go? What happens if everyone hates me? What happens if they mock my accent, or I wear the wrong thing, or if everyone is super smart and I'm not? Or I might get lost and end up in the gym when I should be in maths class or … Can't you home school me or something?"

I put the plate down. I couldn't eat anything.

I put on my stupid uniform and looked in the mirror. My London friends would really laugh at me now. It was a navy-blue dress that looked like a sailor suit. White ankle socks, and black Mary Jane shoes. I had pulled my hair back in a ponytail, but I knew as soon as I stepped outside into the rain it would puff out behind me in a big ball of frizz.

23 **to mock** to make fun of sb nastily

I heard a giggle and turned around. Stevie was standing in my doorway, laughing at my uniform. I threw my hairbrush at him.

Lucky little brat. He was still at primary school, so he didn't even have to wear a uniform. He'd met the neighbours yesterday and one of their sons was his age and loved computer games just as much, so he already had a friend at school.

We got into the car and headed to school. I was too nervous to talk much. Even Mum looked apprehensive.

"You'll be fine, Maggie," she said. "Just be yourself and you'll make stacks of friends in no time, you'll see."

I rolled my eyes at her, "Parents always say that sort of rubbish. It's all your fault. I wouldn't be in this situation except for you and your stupid job."

She tightened her hands on the steering wheel. I could see a muscle twitch in her jaw.

We pulled up at the school. The large white building was big and imposing. It looked cold and unfriendly. There were groups of kids in their uniforms hanging out, talking, and listening to music. I got out at the drop off point and followed a sign pointing me into the office. I tried not to notice a group of girls staring at me as I walked by. One of them whispered something that I couldn't catch as I walked by. I think it was about my shoes.

The office lady, with her grey curls, nodded kindly at me.

"Are you new today, dear? Take a seat here and I'll get someone to take you to your form class."

I sat down and waited.

A cute guy about my age came into the office. He was tall, with tanned skin and curly dark hair.

"Hi, are you Maggie?" he said, his voice friendly.

"Hi," I said, struggling to make eye contact. I swallowed.

---

3 **brat** annoying, often badly-behaved, child – 7 **to head** (verb) to go towards –
8 **apprehensive** worried about sth that might happen – 10 **stacks** a large amount of –
15 **to twitch** to make small uncontrolled movements – 15 **jaw** the lower part of your face that moves when you eat – 17 **imposing** large and important-looking – 30 **to swallow** *(here)* to make a nervous reaction or movement, as if drinking or eating sth

"I'm Joseph. Come with me and I'll show you around."

I picked up my bag and we left the office.

"You're from London, right? Why are you here in Auckland?"

"It's my mum, she got a job, so she made us come. I didn't want to though, no one wants to start a new school when they are fifteen. It's terrifying." 5

Joe smiled at me, "Yeah, I know. I was new too at the beginning of the year, I came down from up north. It's hard leaving all your friends."

I swallowed again. Gosh, he was cute. 10

Once we got out of the main building, the rest of the school looked less impressive. Joseph took me to the small room that was my form class. It was one of a group of three set around a muddy patch of grass. We walked up the steps to the door. I could see a blur of faces through the window. 15

"Alright, you ready?"

I nodded nervously.

He opened the door and about thirty faces stared at me. The teacher stood up and smiled. He was stocky, with too much hair product in his hair. 20

"Welcome, Maggie. Class say hi to Maggie."

I mumbled hi and looked around the faces of the people in the class. A few were smiling at me, but a couple of blonde girls in the front row looked at me slyly, one whispering behind her hand.

The classroom looked untidy, there were papers stacked high 25 on the teacher's desk and chairs piled up in the corner. There were lots of posters on the corkboard, advertising a school fair, babysitting jobs, parties, and an invitation to audition for a TV show. 'NZ's Next Catwalk Queen,' I think it said.

"Where are you from, Maggie?" 30

"I'm from London. Um… in England?" I said wishing I could disappear.

---

15 **blur** sth that is unclear – 19 **stocky** person: short and well-built – 24 **slyly** behaving as if hiding sth or plotting sth

He smiled. "Is that where it is?" he said. "I wasn't sure."

There were laughs from the class.

"Why don't you take a seat?" He pointed to a seat next to two students at the back of the class.

"See ya 'round, Maggie," Joseph closed the door.

I walked, eyes down, past the girls whispering at the front of the class and sat down.

A girl with freckles and a heavy fringe looked at me and smiled.

She said, "I'm Huia and this is Terence."

Terence had black glasses and red spots on his chin.

"London, eh?" said Huia. "Cool, but why? I mean, why would you come from London to here?"

I smiled at Huia, "No choice sadly. My mum got a job here, so here we are."

"And what do you think so far?" asked Terence.

"Honestly?" I said. "I don't know – at this point everything just feels a bit weird and overwhelming."

"Well, this school isn't too bad," said Terence. "Let us tell you all you need to know."

He pointed around the classroom.

"Most kids are nice, except for them."

He nodded at the blonde girls sat at the front of the class. The same girls that whispered as I came in.

"Especially her, she is REALLY not nice," Terence said.

He nodded his head at a pretty girl who was taking photos of herself on her phone. She had blonde hair pulled up into a tight bun, remarkably high cheekbones and her school uniform was tight and short.

"Her name is Serena. Yes, she is gorgeous and yes, she knows it. I'd advise staying away from her."

---

8 **freckles** small brown spots on the skin – 18 **overwhelming** too much to take in or comprehend – 28 **bun** when the hair is drawn back and wound into a circle

"OK," I said. "Good to know. How about the teachers?"

"Well, we are lucky, because Mr Little is one of the better teachers - he's good, mostly. He is crazy about history and rugby."

"I'm taking history," I said.

"Cool," said Huia. "You'll be in his class for that. I'm taking it too."

I said, "But, I don't know much about rugby."

Terence and Huia looked shocked.

"You don't know much about rugby? Rugby is super popular here. I mean, the First Fifteen are like gods."

"What do you mean, the First Fifteen? The First Fifteen what?"

Huia laughed, "The First Fifteen are the best rugby players in the school. They are in the top team. We all go to support them when they play. It's not mandatory, but you know it's one of those things we are expected to do. Joseph, who brought you in, he's in the First Fifteen. He's good. He won a scholarship to play and board at school."

"And he is super-hot, too," added Terence. "I wouldn't say no."

Huia smiled, "But his girlfriend Serena wouldn't be happy with you."

She nodded towards the pretty blonde girl with the camera at the front of the class.

"What sports do they play in London? Soccer?" Terence asked.

"Soccer? What's ... Oh, you mean football. Yes, lots of the kids play football, but at my school people weren't so keen on sport. It was more like art and film making."

Huia shook her head, "I think you are going to find it quite different here."

The day passed quickly. I moved from class to class. Luckily, Huia was in lots of my classes, and she seemed nice, so she was able to show me where to go.

---

14 **mandatory** obligatory – 17 **to board** to live at the school during the school term

They didn't have school lunches here. There was a canteen where you could buy things, but it wasn't like my old school where we all had trays of hot food. Here, people brought lunch boxes with sandwiches, or you could buy food, but it wasn't provided. I bought and ate a bit of a sandwich. It was hard to find something that was vegetarian.

Finally, the last bell rang. It was 3:30 and time to go. Kids started streaming out of the school gates, a blur of navy blue, brown and white. I stood under the tree by the crossing where mum was going to pick me up and waited.

"Hi Maggie," said a voice, "how did you survive your first day?

Joseph was standing at the crossing with Serena from my form class. They were holding hands. Sigh. Serena was so *pretty*. She even walked like a model on the catwalk.

"It was alright, I guess," I said. "It's different."

Serena frowned at me. "What do you mean?' she said.

"It's different," I said, "I mean here you don't have school lunches; you can call your teachers by their first names, you must ask to go to the toilet, people seem crazy about rugby, it rains all the time, the uniform is uncomfortable and SO ugly… it's weird. I mean why is it so ugly?"

I stopped. Serena was still frowning.

"Well, *we* like it," said Serena.

"Oh, I'm not complaining," I said, my voice trailing off.

I probably did sound like I was complaining a bit.

"… it's just different, you know, and I miss my friends and …," I said lamely.

"Whatever," said Serena. "Come on, Joseph."

She walked away.

Joseph gave me an uncomfortable smile, "Sorry about that."

"No, *I'm* sorry – that was a bit of a no-filter moment."

---

11 **to survive** *(here)* to get through a difficult situation successfully – 24 **to trail off** when you finish speaking, to sound uncertain of what you were saying – 27 **lamely** without sounding very confident – 31 **no-filter** when sb doesn't judge correctly whether they should say sth or not

He hurried off after her.

Mum's car pulled in. Stevie was in the back seat, beaming.

"I had the best day, Maggie," he said. "My new school is so cool! We do gardening! I got to catch flies for the class frogs!"

I frowned at him.

"How was your day?" Mum asked.

"It was mostly terrible," I said. "Do I really have to go back tomorrow?"

Was Joseph sympathetic to Maggie in the beginning? How do you know?

Did his attitude change in any way later? Why?

Think about it...

What do you know about the game of rugby? List the main differences between rugby and football/soccer.

Does being good at sports make a student more popular, do you think? What alternatives are there?

Chapter 4

I did, in fact, have to go back the next day, and the day after that, and the day after that. After a while it was OK. Huia and I got on pretty well and we all sat together for lunch. Mostly it got easier.

What didn't get easier was Serena. I must have somehow really offended her on that first day because she'd often glare at me across the classroom. Once, I even heard her mocking my accent.

"All right guv'nor," she said as I walked past, "I'm from London and I don't like it 'ere."

I kept my head down and pretended not to notice.

Huia told me not to worry, "She's mean to everyone, Maggie, even the teachers are scared of her."

So, I tried, but mostly I just really missed London.

I did go to my first rugby match. Our school was playing an all-boys' school. It was a Saturday morning, and for what felt like

---

22 **to offend** to make sb upset by saying or doing sth to them – 22 **to glare** to stare at sb angrily

the first Saturday in forever it wasn't raining. The game was being played on the field at school. Huia and I walked there together.

We went in the front gate, Huia filling me in on the rules.

"So… you can pick the ball up WITH your HANDS?"

"Yes," said Huia, sighing. "Yes, - for the fourth time - it's different from football. Yes, you can pick up the ball with your hands."

She sounded annoyed. "Look, I don't really understand all the rules either, but there are only two that you need to know: don't throw the ball forward and never tackle someone around the neck."

I was surprised by how many people from school were there.

"Oh wow, so it *is* a thing. People do come and watch it," I said to Huia.

"I mean – I know you told me it was, but gosh this would never happen in London. This would never happen in London," Serena was close and repeated what I said in a high-pitched voice. "Is that all you ever say, Maggie? Poor me, this isn't the same as London. I miss my fancy English lifestyle." She looked me up and down, "Oh, and nice shoes," she said sarcastically. "They must be fashionable in London … because they sure aren't fashionable here."

Her friends, the blonde girls that followed her, started laughing.

"That's not very nice," said Huia. "Don't be so mean. Serena, what's your problem?"

"What's *my* problem? What's *her* problem? Why does she have to come over here and complain about everything. Looking down her nose at how we do things here."

"I do not!" I said furiously. "It's just that its different here and I'm still getting used to everything."

---

10 **to tackle** in rugby: to physically throw yourself at a member of the opposing team to try and get the ball off them – 20 **sarcastically** meaning the opposite of what you are saying

"Well, it sure sounds like you are looking down your nose at us. Do me a favour and go back to where you come from. We don't like you and we don't want you here."

She stalked off. Her friends followed her.

Huia looked upset. "Maggie, I'm so sorry. That was super rude."

I said, "Let's just forget about it."

We climbed up the wooden seats and sat down. It was cold. There was a coffee cart and an old food truck selling food. Instead of netted goals like football, there were two 'H' shaped goal posts at either end. There were a lot of people watching the game, at least half the school I'd say. Apparently, this was an important one: our First Fifteen versus the boys' school down the road. The two teams were in a huddle on either end of the field. The referee blew a whistle, and they took their places on the field. I could see Joseph, dressed in his uniform, black hair falling down the front of his face in a triangle.

I smiled. Huia followed my line of sight.

"Oh, *okay*. Like that is it? Now, I think I know why Serena was so mean to you," she said. "You'll be lucky, Serena snapped him up as soon as he got here at the beginning of the year."

I blushed.

"Oh well, he'd never look at me anyway – I'm just a grumpy weirdo from London who doesn't understand rugby."

"Ha, you sure are!" she laughed.

I frowned at her, hurt.

"No, not really, I was only joking. I'm glad your mum decided to bring you here."

I wasn't really listening; I was thinking about Joseph. He did look very handsome in his rugby uniform, running up and down the field. I wondered if he could ever fancy me.

---

4 **to stalk off** to walk away proudly, in a superior fashion – 13 **huddle** (noun) a small tight group – 19 **to snap up** *(here)* to quickly take the opportunity to have as a boyfriend – 21 **to blush** to go red from embarrassment – 22 **grumpy** bad-tempered – 23 **weirdo** strange person

I wasn't unattractive. I mean I'm not like a model like Serena, I'm just normal looking. Normal figure, normal size, normal face. The only thing that is different is that I have a big mass of brown curly hair which has a life of its own. It's thick with ringlets and can very easily look like a haystack unless I tame it. I've got normal brown eyes. Sometimes I get pimples around my hairline.

The whistle blew and the boys raced up and down the field. There was a lot of running, pushing, and throwing each other to the ground. As far as I could tell, it was a bit like a massive game of tag. But instead of tagging each other, the players had to pull each other to the ground and get the ball off the other team.

The crowd was vocal, with parents shouting from the sidelines. Then the referee blew his whistle – and it was half time. The score was 27 – 18.

Huia suggested I get hot chips. "Hot chips at a rugby game! A true Kiwi Saturday morning experience!"

On the way back I walked past Joseph. He looked muddy and sweaty. He was drinking out of a water bottle.

"Hi Maggie," he said.

He smiled and his eyes crinkled a little at the corners. "Enjoying your first rugby game?"

"Yeah, although I'm still not sure what's going on."

He laughed, "Well, keep watching, I'm sure you'll figure it out."

"I'm sure I will too! It actually seems faster and more interesting than football."

He grinned, "I bet your boyfriend in London wouldn't like you saying that."

"I don't have a boyfriend," I said.

He looked at me and was about to say something, but - the referee blew the whistle again.

"Ok, got to go," he said, putting the water bottle down.

---

5 **to tame** *(here)* to be able to control hair or style it properly – 6 **pimple** spot – 12 **vocal** loud, noisy – 20 **to crinkle** to form little lines

"See you, have a good game, … um, break a leg. Whoops, I mean - not really!" I said.

He laughed and jogged back onto the field.

I turned around and found myself face to face with Serena.

"You know he's MY boyfriend, right? You need to stay away from him. You and your stupid English accent and your stupid English clothes."

She stood close to me, pushing her face into mine.

"Oh my god," I said, "I don't want to steal your boyfriend. We were just chatting."

"Well, don't," she said and pushed me.

It hurt. I clenched my fists, my face red.

I pushed her back.

"Don't touch me," I said.

I leaned towards her and said through my teeth. "I'm not trying to steal your boyfriend, we were only talking because he is a nice person, and he was being nice to me. Something *you* could learn about."

I pushed her again.

She looked surprised. "Get your hands off me," she shouted.

Heads turned and everyone looked at me.

"She pushed me first," I said. Shaking my head, I walked back to where Huia was sitting.

I hate this stupid place and its stupid people. I can't wait to go back to London.

---

12 **to clench your fists** to hold your hands as if to hit sb, in anger

What is Maggie referring to when she says, 'This would never happen in London?'

Why does Serena dislike Maggie so much?

Think about it...

Which sports do you play at school? Are there any other sports you would like to try?

Do you prefer team sports or solo sports? Why?

Chapter 5

It was the last week of term, a week after the rugby fiasco.

After the fight I had with Serena, I went home and told Mum about how I hated it here, and how much I wanted to go back to London. She had sighed and looked worried. She wanted to call my teacher, and talk to him, but I made her promise not to. Stevie of course, was enjoying himself here. Sometimes I wondered why my life was so much harder than his.

Now it was Wednesday, the week before the holidays.

Everyone in the class was excited because we were going on a class trip. We had to get to school early with clothes for two days and a sleeping bag. We were going to visit a marae up in Waitangi. A marae is a meeting house for Māori and the one in Waitangi is particularly important because .... well for some reason. I was a bit behind on my reading for history.

---

18 **fiasco** mess, disaster

Despite hating everything, I felt excited. It was the first time I'd been out of stupid Auckland.

The bus pulled up outside the front of the main school building. All the kids taking history got on. There was the usual shouting and pushing to get the seats in the back. I got a seat with Huia.

"Hi Maggie," said a voice and Joseph said down behind me with his friend Tāne.

Huia giggled at me.

"Hi," I said then looked out the window, so he didn't see my face reddening.

"I'm super excited to go up north," he said. "It's where my hapu is from."

I didn't really know what he meant.

"Oh, I'm Ngāti Kawa," he said to my blank look. "That's my iwi."

"Your what?"

"My iwi – it means my tribe. My family come from up north. It's my tūrangawaewae."

"What's tūrangawaewae?" I couldn't pronounce the words very well.

"That means my place of belonging. It's my homeland, where I feel most at home and most connected."

"Oh, right," I said uncomfortably. Maybe I should have read a bit more about NZ history.

The bus was hot. As we drove out of Auckland over the Harbour Bridge, I realised I didn't feel very well. I put my headphones in, listened to music and tried to keep my eyes fixed on a distant point. Apparently, that's the way to stop feeling sick. It was fine when we were on the motorway, the roads were smooth and straight, mostly. The scenery was lush and green. It looked like English scenery, cows, sheep, fences – but

18 **tribe** a particular social and ancestral family group – 29 **apparently** seemingly – 31 **lush** with lots of green leafy plants

occasionally I'd see stands of trees that didn't look English –
brighter colours, spikier leaves. The land looked rougher too, like
it hadn't been smoothed out as by people or something.

We stopped for a toilet break and to have morning tea.

"Are you OK, Maggie?" asked Huia as we were getting off the
bus.

"You look a bit pale."

"Yes, I just always get a bit of motion sickness. I'm normally
OK if the roads are nice and straight."

Joseph overheard me talking.

"I guess you haven't ever driven over the Brynderwyns, then?"
he said. "I hate to break it to you, but it gets worse from now on."

I smiled uneasily. "I'm usually ok, but it's just so hot in the bus."

We got out and had ten minutes to stretch our legs and get
some fresh air. Some of the kids went to the loo. Joe had a chat
with the driver. Huia and I sat on the bench, and I concentrated
on breathing slowly.

Mr Little blew his whistle. "Back on the bus everyone please!"

Kids came out of the petrol station and slowly started filing
back in. The bus started up again.

The air felt quite a lot cooler. Thank goodness. My stomach
didn't feel anywhere near as upset.

Joseph leant forward from the seat behind. "Is that a bit better?
I asked the bus driver to turn up the air conditioning."

"It's so much better. Thank you."

Huia looked at me, then she looked at Joseph and then she
giggled. My face reddened.

I put my headphones back in again and checked my phone.
There was a message there from Mum:

'Have a good time sweetheart – hope you can sleep!'

There was also a message from Stevie: 'Mum says we are going
to get dumplings while you are away! Ha-ha sucks to be you.'

---

3 **to smooth out** to make sth flat – 19 **to file back in** to go back into a place in a line

40

I sent him back a quick message telling him he was a brat.

My phone pinged again. It was a message, but the sender came up as unknown.

"Why don't you go back to England. No one likes you."

My heart started to beat faster and my phone shook in my hands.

I looked around the bus – was it one of my classmates who sent me the message? No one was looking at me, as far as I could tell. A bunch of kids in the four-seater next to me were playing cards. Joe looked like he was asleep, Huia was staring out the window with her headphones on. Everyone else was either laughing, talking, or sleeping.

I looked back at my phone again.

The message was still there. I grabbed the paper bag out of the front seat.

Huia looked at me.

"Oh no," she said. "Are you going to be sick?"

I nodded. "I feel awful. Can you get the bus driver to stop?"

She called down the bus to the teacher. "Mr Little? Maggie is sick."

Mr Little turned around and looked at me. He sighed. Everyone on the bus also turned and looked at me. Even the cards players stopped.

"What's wrong now, Maggie?" He called up the bus.

In response, I vomited into the paper bag I was holding.

"Ugh. Okay." Holding on to the corners of the seats he made his way down to the driver and asked the driver to pull over.

All the kids on the bus were staring at me as I walked down the aisle, Huia following me.

I climbed down off the bus, then went and crouched in the trees on the side of the road. I threw up a couple of times. A tear or two rolled down my face. Huia passed me a bottle of water.

---

25 **to vomit** to be physically sick

"You poor thing. I thought you were going to be OK."

"Yeah, sorry," I mumbled. "I thought I was going to be OK too, but then I got this text message and it really upset me and just make me feel worse."

I showed her my phone.

"I don't know who sent it. But I think I can guess."

Why didn't Maggie understand the majority of the Māori words?

What made Maggie feel worse on the bus?

Think about it...

How important is it to know about the history of the place you are visiting? Give reasons.

Together with language, what else forms an important part of a people's culture?

---

2 **to mumble** to speak quietly, with difficulty

Chapter 6

I managed to not throw up for the rest of the drive, I closed my
eyes and listened to soothing music. About lunch time we pulled
into the Bay of Islands and drove into Paihia.

The Bay of Islands was beautiful. Bright blue water, islands,
people lying on the sand, yellow ferries going everywhere. The
colours were amazing. The green of the trees against the blue
and the yellow sand and the sparkling water. We pulled into the
campsite and piled off the bus.

"Right," said Mr Little, standing up at the front of the bus,
holding his beloved clipboard. "This is the plan. Eat your lunch
now – under the trees and then after that you have time to go to
the museum. Tonight, we will have a hāngi and tomorrow we will
go to the marae for a pōwhiri."

"What's a hāngi and a pōwhiri?" I asked Huia.

"A hāngi is a traditional Māori meal, its cooked underground –
usually pork and kumara and potatoes. It's delicious. A pōwhiri is
a welcome onto the marae. There is a call, speeches and a waiata."

"That's a song," she added as I looked confused.

"I can't sing," I said in terror.

"Don't worry," she sighed. "We all sing together. Maggie, didn't
you do *any* of the reading?"

After lunch we looked around the museum.

I didn't know this, (probably because I hadn't done the reading)
but Waitangi is special because in February 1840 it was the
site for the signing of a treaty by Māori and William Hobson,
representing the British Crown. The Treaty of Waitangi is the
founding document for Aotearoa NZ – but there was lots of
dodginess when it came to the translations, so the Māori chiefs
thought they were signing different things.

---

2 **soothing** relaxing – 8 **to pile off** to leave a bus, etc in a large group – 10 **clipboard**
a small flat board holding pieces of paper to write on – 25 **treaty** an official agreement
between countries – 26 **to represent** to stand in place of – 27 **founding** (adj) that
represents the formal beginning of sth – 28 **dodginess** containing unclear or false
information

That lead to land theft, and terrible things in general happening to Māori – which is why there are protests every year on Waitangi Day.

…

We were sleeping in dormitories at the campsite. There was a big open room with bunk beds for the girls and across a patch of grass the same space for the boys, and the toilet and shower block on the third side of the grass. There were wooden picnic tables in the middle.

Next to the picnic table was a large pit, where the hāngi was cooking. It smelt great and I realised how hungry I was. At about 7pm they pulled it up, peeled back the foil wrappings and placed it on the tables. We lined up to get something – but as I got closer, I could see large chunks of pork, all mixed in together with the sweet potatoes and corn. Oh no.

I sidled up to Mr Little and quietly tried to get his attention.

"Um, Sir? Is there anything that isn't cooked in with the pork? It's just – I'm a vegetarian."

Mr Little looked annoyed. He checked the clipboard he was holding.

"Really? I'm sorry, Maggie, but that wasn't on your form?"

"Oh, I don't know," I said. "I think my mum must have filled it out … she has been pretty busy lately." I trailed off.

"Well, we didn't cater for you, because we didn't know. Next time *you* need to check." He sounded annoyed. "I think I've got a couple of muesli bars, which will have to do I'm afraid."

"Ok, thanks, that's fine. Thanks," I put my head down and walked back to the girls' dorm room trying not to make eye contact with anyone. I sat on my bed in the room by myself and ate the muesli bars. They tasted like cardboard.

---

1 **theft** stealing – 14 **chunks** large pieces – 14 **pork** the meat from a pig – 16 **to sidle up** to approach sb quietly and carefully – 22 **to fill out** to complete (a form etc) with the necessary details

After my dinner of muesli bars, it was time to get ready for sleep. We took our toiletries and changed in the shower block. I had brought my cutest pjs, but I walked quickly back to our dorm room. It was weird being around school people in my sleep wear.

"Cute pjs," called Huia from the dormitory deck, obviously not bothered at all about my sense of embarrassment.

"Joseph's looking cute in his, too." She nodded across the camp site. I took a quick look. He was lying on his back on the boy's deck talking to a couple of friends.

"Ha," said Huia. "You've totally got a crush."

"But Maggie," her tone changed. "What are you going to do about that text message?"

I felt queasy again.

"I think I'll just leave it. If it happens again. I'll talk to Mr. Little."

Eventually the lights went out. All I could hear were noises – snoring, breathing, laughing. I'm never going to get to sleep I thought. Until suddenly the sunlight came through and I was awake.

…

Please leave shoes here!
THANKS

---

10 **to have a crush on sb** to really like sb – 13 **queasy** not feeling very well, feeling sick

After breakfast (thankfully with a vegetarian option), it was time to go across to the marae. We walked across the big green lawn. There was a waka (canoe) that was a replica of the one sailed to New Zealand hundreds of years ago from Hawaiki. There were a couple of tall trees spreading their branches across the ground.

We were welcomed onto the marae by a pōwhiri. The call sounded ancient and sent shivers up my spine. I looked across at Joseph. He looked comfortable and relaxed. He saw me looking at him and smiled.

There was a challenge, and then they sang a song, and then we sang a song – a waiata. Everyone else seemed to know it. I tried my best to lip sync. Then they signalled for us to go onto the marae.

I was thinking about the horrible text message though, and not paying attention when we got closer to the door. I put my backpack down and walked through the door.

"Excuse me! Miss! Miss!"

I heard someone calling behind me, but I didn't think anyone was talking to me. I went inside and started looking around. The roof inside the marae was high, with a long piece of wood, like a spine holding up two sides of the ceiling. There were drawings and carvings in red and white on the four walls. In the front corner next to the door was a small window.

"Miss, WAIT!" One of the people who welcomed us hurried up to me.

"Miss, you have still got your shoes on," he said very loudly. "You absolutely cannot do that. This is a sacred place where we respect our tūpuna and we don't allow shoes."

His voice was loud, and it carried and the conversations around me stopped suddenly. Heads turned to look at me and I saw two of

---

1 **option** alternative – 3 **replica** sth that has been made to look identical to the original – 8 **to send shivers up your spine** to make sb feel excited or frightened – 23 **carving** a pattern cut in stone or wood – 28 **sacred** respected in a particular religion, holy

my classmates' whisper something behind their hands at each other. Huia was looking at me with a shocked expression on her face.

I could feel my face going red.

"Oh my god, I'm so sorry," I said. I bent down and kicked off my shoes. "I can't believe I didn't realise; sorry! I'm so sorry! I was just thinking about something else."

"God, Maggie," said Huia, "look at all those shoes out the front. I can't believe you didn't see them. Open your eyes, will you? Stop being so self-absorbed. It's so offensive!"

My face reddened. Head down, I took my shoes outside. I put them down carefully, toes touching with the rest of the shoes. Huia was right, there were so many shoes here. Everyone must have taken their shoes off. How could I not have noticed?

> What was the problem connected with the Treaty of Waitangi?

> Why did Maggie not take off her shoes when she entered the marae?

Think about it...

> Why do people become vegetarians? How do you feel about that?

> Describe a typical feast day in your country. What do you like most about it?

9 **self-absorbed** only interested in your own feelings and experiences – 9 **offensive** very rude

Chapter 7

Back in Auckland for the rest of the last week of term, I kept my head down. Huia wasn't speaking to me. Serena kept laughing whenever I walked past, and even Terence seemed uncomfortable around me. I was glad when it was Friday and the beginning of the school holidays.

Unfortunately, Mum had organised a holiday trip for us. It was cold and raining and we were up early on the Saturday to pack our things into the car.

"It's a bit stupid to be going to the beach for the weekend in weather like this, isn't it?" I asked Mum.

She looked at me, sighed and rolled her eyes.

Stevie, of course didn't care about the rain. He was just excited. He was dancing around the hallway dressed in his bright red swimsuit shorts.

"I'm going to swim in the sea!" he said, jumping up and down.

Mum got me to hold her phone in the car. The little tinny voice of the Sat Nav directed us towards how to get out of the city. After about an hour, we were in the Waikato.

"It's very flat," said Stevie.

It was. Green and flat with the occasional group of cows and tall hedges bordering lots of flat fields.

"Look over there," Mum nodded her head towards a range of mountains in the distance. There was a big grey cloud over it. "That's where we are going."

"That's where we are heading? Mum! It looks even worse than here."

I sighed. Mum sighed too and looked sideways at me.

"Come *on* Maggie, you promised. Try to be a little bit more enthusiastic, please. I know it's your hormones…"

I groaned.

" …. But this teenage disinterest is really boring."

We drove over a bridge. It had a large Māori statue guarding the entrance, holding a big stick. Stevie pointed at it. I looked a bit closer and saw the statue had a large bare bottom. We both started sniggering.

Eventually, we pulled into the small town where we were going to spend our weekend. Mum had hired an apartment for the weekend. Set back off the beach it had polished wooden floors, soft grey woollen blankets, and abstract art on the walls. And the walls weren't beige! Bliss! We unpacked and ate lunch.

Mum consulted her phone. "Ok!" she said mysteriously. "Get your swimsuit on! It's time!"

"Time for what? To freeze to death?" I asked. "Do you really expect me to go outside in this weather."

"Yes," she said, "I do. Come on, hurry up."

---

1 **tinny** having a thin metallic sound – 20 **to snigger** to laugh at sth or sb, often unkindly or through embarrassment – 27 **to consult** *(here)* to look at sth for information

I shrugged my shoulders and gave up. Fine, if she wanted us to catch our deaths from cold. So be it.

I put on my swimsuit. She gave us each a spade to carry.

It was raining hard, and it was surprisingly cold. The sand was fine and white. We waded through a small rocky stream and walked about five minutes along the beach. I kept trying to stop – but Mum kept looking at her phone, waving me on. "No, not here, Maggie. Not here."

I gritted my teeth. This was tedious. My hair was busting out of its ponytail in the rain.

We walked on a little further, around the corner. Stevie was down by the water's edge, playing his favourite game of 'avoid the tide.' He had explained the rules to me once. Essentially if you can avoid the water, you win. If the water gets you, the water wins. It involved shrieking and running backwards and forwards, and usually resulted in Mum getting angry at him for getting all his clothes wet.

It is quite a fun game, but of course, at 15, I'm too old to play. Well, too old to play when there are cute surfers around anyway.

There were a couple of other groups of people further down the beach. Mum seemed to be walking towards them.

"Mum," I said, "there's a whole beach here. Why are we crowding those people out?"

"You'll see," she smiled. "Ok. I think we can try here."

She put her bag and towel down on a dry bit of sand further towards the rocks, then walked down to the water's edge, spade in hand. "Come on," she said. "Let's dig."

"Um. Ok…. Ay," I said half-heartedly following her lead. "What are we digging for? I think I'm a little old to make a sandcastle, don't you think?"

---

1 **to shrug my shoulders** to move your shoulders up and down to show that you don't care – 3 **spade** a tool you dig with – 5 **to wade** to walk through shallow water – 9 **to grit my teeth** to show determination to carry on despite difficulties – 9 **tedious** boring and tiring – 13 **tide** the movement of the sea coming in and going out – 15 **to shriek** to shout loudly in excitement

Stevie produced his plastic spade and started digging too. The sand was damp and heavy and quite hard to turn. We dug in silence then, a little water started bubbling up.

There was a little steam too.

The water was hot!

We dug a bathtub shaped hole and jumped into it. The water was surprisingly hot - on the edge of too hot. Stevie made it his mission to fill up cold water from the sea with his little red bucket. He ran backwards and forwards, filling it up and pouring it into our sandy hot water beach bathtub. Mum and I sat down. The water was lovely and warm. The sea was grey, blue, and reached as far as I could see.

"This is amazing," said Mum. "You can't do this in London."

I sighed.

She grinned at me. "Alright then, what do you miss the most?"

I opened my mouth and it all spilled out. I talked about school, the problems with Serena at the rugby, my awful embarrassment at the marae and how I just didn't feel like I fitted in here.

Mum listened and nodded.

"I'm sorry it's so tough for you," she said. "I really didn't think it would be this hard."

I felt a bit bad for making her feel so bad.

"Also, you know your hormones are all a bit skewed because you are a teenager, so sometimes things feel worse than they are."

I rolled my eyes. "Mum, stop being such a menopause doctor."

"Ok, fair enough. Well …. let's try to re-frame it … Is there anything good at all about being here?"

I tilted my head back and got a raindrop in my eye. I thought hard. I could tell Mum really wanted to hear something positive.

"I really like Huia; we get on well – well we did before the marae. And the classes are good, I guess. I like how relaxed the kids are."

---

8 **mission** an important job or a duty – 18 **to fit in** to be accepted in a new situation –
23 **skewed** not normal or as they should be – 28 **to tilt** to move slightly

Mum smiled.

"What about you, Mum, what do you like about being here?"

Mum opened her mouth to answer and then looked down to the water's edge. Stevie's bucket was there, upturned. Stevie wasn't there.

She scrambled out of the hot water hole, water streaming off her. She ran down to the water's edge.

"Stevie, where are you?"

I followed close behind.

The people near us looked up. I ran over to them. I was racing but the world moved in slow motion.

"Have you seen my little brother? That's his bucket."

They shook their heads. "We'll help you look," said the dad in the group.

Mum waded into the water, eyes scanning the water.

"Stevie, where are you?"

The waves were splashing on the shore. But there was no sign of Stevie. Water splashed around my feet as I ran towards the lifeguard flags.

"My brother," I said breathing fast. "He was here, but we can't see him? He was just filling up his bucket with water and bringing it to us." I waved in the direction where we were. Mum's voice, loud and scared, was echoing across the beach. A crowd of people stood near the water's edge.

The lifeguards looked concerned. They radioed someone; then, moving very quickly dragged the lifeboat out to the water. Pulling hard on the motor, it roared into life. The boat went over the waves and headed towards where Mum was standing.

"Stevie!" Mum's voice sounded strained. I ran back towards her, eyes scanning the water. The lifeboat, yellow and red, zigzagged back and forth, lifeguards looking intently into the water. The surfers paddled over to help look too. The people on the water's edge fanned out. I held tightly onto Mum.

---

24 **concerned** worried – 29 **to zigzag** to move to the left and then to the right – 32 **to fan out** to spread out over a bigger area

54

She was shaking. Time seemed to stop. The water came in and out. The waves splashing Mum and I as we stood, arms around each other, looking out at the sea.

There was a shout. One of the surfers lent over and pulled a small figure, wearing red shorts onto his board. Mum's legs gave way. She sat heavily down in the water. The small figure didn't move.

The lifeguards pulled Stevie from the surfboard onto his boat. One started giving Stevie mouth to mouth. The other lifeguard steered the boat back to the shore.

A siren sounded in the background. Mum and I ran to meet the boat.

The boat stopped on the sand.

"Come on," muttered the lifeguard as he continued the breathing and the compression.

---

32 **compression** *(here)* pushing down hard on a victim's chest

Suddenly Stevie coughed and spat out a large amount of water. He
started crying. The lifeguard gently lifted him out of the boat and put
him into the recovery position on the sand. Mum and I crouched
down next to him. Mum stroked his forehead. He coughed and
shivered. There was a cut on his head and a scratch on his leg.

The ambulance arrived. In a blur of synchronised action, the
paramedics wheeled a stretcher onto the beach. They checked
him over.

"Ok, we'll take him to the hospital in Thames," said the
paramedics.

"We'll follow you," said Mum, white-faced. She ran up the
beach, in her swimsuit, towards our holiday apartment.

I followed, feeling sick at the sight of Stevie's little body
wheeled away on a stretcher.

> Why did Maggie's mum insist on taking them to the beach even when the weather was bad?

> How do you think the accident with Stevie happened?

Think about it...

Do you think Maggie's constant lack of enthusiasm
for certain activities is typical teenage behaviour?
Why is that?

How important do you think honesty
is in relationships?

---

1 **to spit out** to blow liquid from your mouth – 4 **to crouch** to lower your body close to
the ground – 6 **synchronised** when actions happen at the same time

Chapter 8

Mum didn't talk in the car. Her face was white and strained. I could tell she was stopping herself from speeding – she stayed exactly at the same speed at the speed level required.

The ambulance quickly disappeared ahead of us, light flashing, siren ringing.

"Maggie, can you check how long it will take to get to the Thames hospital?" Mum asked.

I looked at the online map, "It looks like an hour, an hour ten."

Mums' lips tightened and she pressed down on the accelerator.

I wiped my face and tried not to think about the worst.

We made it in 50 minutes. The Thames hospital was a small four-storied white building, sat squarely on the flat streets of the small country town. Mum parked, took a deep breath, and got out of the car. She looked very tired.

We walked up to the reception. My legs and arms were shaking.

---

19 **required** *(here)* as stated by law – 26 **accelerator** the pedal you use to increase speed

Mum was talking to the receptionist.

"My son was bought in here - he was at Hot Water beach. " Her voice wavered. "Can you tell me where he is?"

"Yes," the receptionist said. "Gosh, you must have driven here fast. I'll take you to him directly."

My heart was beating fast as we walked down the long corridor which smelled faintly of cleaning products. A man wearing scrubs and a mask approached us. "Hi, are you Stevie's mum?"

Mum nodded, her hand on her throat.

"Well, he's doing very well," the man said. "He is up and talking and I don't think there is any permanent damage – he has had a bit of a shock, and he probably won't want to go swimming again for a while … but we managed to get all the water out of him."

Mum went pale, crumpled up and dropped to the floor. The man looked surprised.

"Oh dear," he said. "I wasn't expecting that. Nurse!" he called.
"Can you come and give me a hand here?"

They lifted Mum up onto some chairs, and she bent over and put her head between her knees.

"I'm OK," she said.

They took us into his room. Stevie was sitting up, propped up on pillows wearing a hospital gown. He looked small and pale, his eyes red. He burst into tears when he saw us.

"I didn't mean to go into the water," he said. "I was just playing and then the water dragged me out."

Mum wrapped her arms around him. "It's OK," she said.

They hugged tightly a moment. I watched, feeling awkward.

"Come here Maggie," Mum turned and wrapped her arms around me too. We all stood there for a moment, breathing together.

Stevie lifted his head from Mum's neck.

---

3 **to waver** to shake slightly – 8 **scrubs** hospital gown – 11 **permanent** long-term, lasting forever – 14 **to crumple up** to collapse – 25 **to drag** to pull with force

"I'm SO HUNGRY," Stevie said. "Can I get something from the vending machine?"

Mum laughed.

"Maggie will get you something," she said.

As I was putting in the numbers for Stevie's favourite chocolate bar into the vending machine, I thought about how my life would be without Stevie. He wasn't that bad, well - except when he was hungry. He was fun mostly. *He* had tried to enjoy it here, even though I knew he was missing home. *He* hadn't made enemies of all his friends by being too self-absorbed. *He* wasn't hard work and teenage and 'boring.'

I picked up the chocolate bar from the bottom of the machine and squared my shoulders. Mum and Stevie were curled up on the hospital bed watching something on TV. It cut to the ads just as I came in the door.

"Are you NZ's Next Catwalk Queen?"

A beautiful man, with a very full upper lip was pointing out from the TV. He winked at the camera.

"Is it YOU we are looking for?" he asked.

Mum muted the TV as I came in.

"Here you go," I tossed the chocolate bar at Stevie.

"One chocolate bar reward for not dying."

"Maggie!" said Mum.

"Just joking," I said.

"Look, I've just had a bit of an epi… epi…, damn, what's the word?"

I googled it on my phone.

"Epiphany! I've just had an epiphany!" I said.

"I know I've been a pain to be around. I'm going to sort it out."

Mum and Stevie looked at each other.

"About time," said Stevie, mouth full of chocolate.

---

20 **to mute** to turn the sound off – 28 **epiphany** a moment of sudden understanding

What happened to Maggie's mum when she heard that Stevie was going to be OK after his accident?

What was the 'epiphany' that Maggie referred to?

Think about it…

Sometimes we only change our way of thinking when something bad happens. Why is that?

Siblings don't always see eye to eye. Can you think of some ways to avoid conflict between them?

Chapter 9

It was the Monday, the start of the final school term.

I hadn't heard from Huia since we'd got back from the school trip up north. But, in my efforts to be less self-absorbed I decided to try to talk to her, rather than just being grumpy and annoyed about it. WWSD was my new motto. (What would Stevie do?)

Mum dropped me off at school. There were kids milling around outside, waiting for their friends. I saw Terence waiting by the front gate.

I walked over towards him. "How are you? How was your holiday?"

"Yeah, not bad," he said. "I had a lazy time not doing very much at all. Took a few photos. How about you?"

"Mine was OK," I said. "A bit too eventful."

I told him about Stevie's mishap.

---

24 **to mill around** to hang around in large numbers – 31 **eventful** full of interesting things happening – 32 **mishap** accident

"Hey," I said, "have you seen Huia, have you spoken to her at all? She hasn't responded to any of my texts."

"Really?" said Terence. "That doesn't sound like her. I didn't see her over the holidays though."

"I know right, I didn't realise I upset her so much. I mean in my defence it was a totally honest mistake. I didn't know, and I didn't realise it would be so offensive."

Terence looked at me.

"Yeah, but Maggie, that's the problem, isn't it? You didn't know, but *why* didn't you know? It's basic NZ 101 really. If you hadn't been so stuck in your own head, talking, and thinking about London so much, you would have known. You just need to stop being so arrogant."

How rude. I opened my mouth to retaliate. But then I thought … WWSD?

Terence rubbed his forehead.

"I don't mean to upset you," he said, "but I think it's probably worth knowing."

"No, it's fine," I said slowly. "I get it. I'd had that realisation already anyway with my family. But I hadn't realised I'd been such hard work to be around with you guys either. I think I need to talk Huia."

The bell rang and all the kids who'd been milling around the front gate stood up and moved towards the school building. The grass had just been cut and the sun was shining. Terence and I headed towards math class.

We went inside the classroom and headed down the back to where our group of three usually sat.

Huia came in and sat down. She nodded briefly at me. She didn't look happy.

---

6 **in my defence** sth you say to protect yourself from criticism – 13 **arrogant** a sense of being superior – 14 **to retaliate** to reply in the same way – 19 **realisation** understanding

I said, "Look can I talk to you? I know I've been awful, and honestly; you've been nothing but good to me, but I really want to apologise."

Huia looked worried. I took a deep breath and continued.

"I haven't been a nice person to be around. I was so upset about moving from London, and so certain I wouldn't enjoy it, I don't think I've been all that nice. I don't think I've given Auckland a chance. I am so sorry about what happened at the marae, I really didn't do it on purpose, I was just in my own head too much."

Huia looked surprised.

"Wow," she said. "Where did all this internal reflection come from? Has someone stolen Maggie? Is it really you?"

She smiled, but then she took a deep breath.

"But seriously, yes, it has been hard to be friends with you. It's like you think we aren't as good as you somehow because we aren't from London. But we are just as good, better even! Anyway, I think you could have a great time here if you just let yourself relax a bit."

I nodded. I told her about what happened to Stevie over the school holidays.

"… and it just made me think, he doesn't wander around feeling grumpy. He just has an enjoyable time. And I want to be like that, too."

"So can we be friends again?" I asked.

Huia looked thoughtful.

"Sure," she said, "but there are going to be conditions. No more comparing things to London. You have to learn more about NZ."

Then, she opened a textbook and pulled out a pen from her school bag. Motioning me to be quiet, she started writing. For all of math class and the next three classes she paid little attention

---

9 **on purpose** deliberately, wanting to – 12 **internal reflection** deep thinking –
27 **conditions** certain things that must be done

to what we were supposed to be doing. She just concentrated on writing. Occasionally she'd scribble something out, or tear a bit of paper out, or flip her hair out of her eyes impatiently. Every time I tried to look at what she was doing she'd wave me away impatiently. I tried to be patient but eventually it was too much for me.

"What are you *doing?*" I asked.

She looked surprised. "I'm trying to fix your life, Maggie! I've written down all your problems and now I'm coming up with solutions."

Terence grinned. "Didn't she tell you her parents are psychologists? Once she has decided to work her magic on you, you'll never get away. Be afraid, Maggie, be very afraid."

She shushed him and kept writing. Then, about halfway through lunch, she suddenly sat up and said, "Right, I've got it!"

"Come with me, Maggie. Now!"

She leapt up off the field where we were sitting and raced off in the direction of our form class.

"What?" I said following her. "Where are you going?"

She ran up the stairs and raced past Mr Little who looked half asleep in a pile of papers on his desk.

"It was here somewhere," she muttered to herself scanning the corkboard.

She started tearing off the pieces of paper on the walls. Assessments, opportunities, dog walking, babysitting brochures…

"Got it," she said. She held up a piece of paper she'd torn off the corkboard.

"Oh, thank goodness," she said. "We've still got time. It hasn't started yet!

"Ok Maggie, I think this piece of paper and Terence's camera are the answers to all your problems."

---

2 **to scribble sth out** to correct sth untidily and roughly – 25 **assessment** school report, marksheet

How did Maggie's new motto of WWSD affect her attitude towards Huia?

What does Terence mean when he says 'NZ 101'?

Think about it...

When we go to a different country, as Maggie did, we often make comparisons. Have you been to another country, and if so, what comparisons did you make between that country and your own?

Sometimes an apology is necessary to remedy a bad situation. Do you find it easy or difficult to apologise? Why?

Chapter 10

It was the next day. I still didn't know what Huia's conditions were – or why she so manically pulled things off the corkboard in our classroom, but I guess we were friends now, so I didn't care. I knew Terence knew, so maybe I'd be able to get it out of him.

We were all in form class. Kids sitting at desks together, some scrolling through their phones, some reading textbooks, some pretending to listen to Mr Little who was at the front of the class trying to sound important reading the school messages on his clipboard.

There was noise outside, the sounds of a group of people walking towards our classroom. I saw a drone with a camera slowly rising and filming outside the window. The kids in the class stopped looking at their phones and rushed to the window. Mr Little looked surprised. He checked his clipboard.

---

19 **manically** in an excited way – 28 **drone** an aerial vehicle like a flying robot, operated from the ground

---

"Um, I haven't been notified that anything is happening today," he said.

We pushed our way to the window and looked out. On the grass in front of us was the beautiful man with the full lips from the reality show 'NZ Next Catwalk Queen.' He was standing in front of a camera, talking, and pointing at our classroom.

"Oh. My. God.," said Terence, from beside me. "Huia, you work fast."

Huia smiled. "It was your photos that did it, Terence."

"Oh my god, it's Kevin!" shrieked the girl on the other side of me. "What is HE doing here?"

Mr Little looked confused.

He opened the door and called. "Excuse me, what is going on?"

Kevin turned his megawatt light bulb smile on Mr Little. Gosh, Kevin was good-looking. Even though I was sure Mr Little was straight, I could see his knees buckling under that full blown beam.

"It's Mr Little, right?" said Kevin, carefully angling himself so the camera got them both in.

"Yes," said Mr Little, "but I'm not sure – I mean I don't know if you are allowed to be here?"

Kevin laughed, "Don't you know who I am?"

Mr Little looked a bit bemused.

"I'm Kevin MJ – the host of NZ's Next Catwalk Queen. Now we have been informed, by a little 'bird'..."

He turned around and winked at the camera,

"… that there is a potential Next Catwalk Queen contender in your very classroom."

Kevin said, "Do you have a Serena Jones in your classroom?"

There was an audible intake of breath.

"Wow!" said someone.

---

16 **buckle** to lose strength, to become weak – 23 **bemused** confused – 27 **contender** sb who takes part in a competition – 30 **audible** easily heard – 30 **intake of breath** a sudden act of breathing in, through shock

"Go Serena!" said someone else.

"Of course, it's bloody Serena," we heard someone else mutter.

Serena looked surprised at first. But then, she smiled. You could almost see her head swelling. She checked herself in her phone camera and slowly walked to the door of the classroom. She waved from the top of the stairs.

"Like the Queen," giggled Terence.

Then calling out 'Hi Kevin' in a calm, measured tone, she walked insouciantly down the stairs towards the camera, like she'd been planning it all along.

Kevin's eyes widened slightly.

"Well, we've found her!" he said to the camera, "The newest contender for NZ's Next Catwalk Queen. And isn't she stunning?"

He pulled Serena into the shot and placed his arm around her. Then he pointed at the camera.

"But we still need more people! She hasn't won … yet.

He winked at the camera.

"Are you NZ's next catwalk queen? Is it YOU we are looking for?"

And then he said, 'AND … cut.'

In a bustle of noise and energy, Serena was hustled off the field to the principal's office.

"But I don't get it," Terence said. "How does this fit into your master plan, Huia?"

"Watch and learn little caterpillar," said Huia. "Watch and learn."

---

4 **to swell** *(here)* when your sense of self-importance increases – 9 **insouciantly** appearing not to care – 21 **bustle** confusion – 21 **to hustle** to take sb somewhere in a hurry

What do we understand about Mr Little from this chapter?

What does Kevin mean when he says 'a little bird …'?

Think about it…

What do you think of reality shows? Would you ever take part in one? Why?/Why not?

How will Serena's participation in the reality show fit into Huia's plan?

Chapter 11

And that was that.

Serena didn't come back that day. Or the next. School was so much better with her gone!

The gossip slowly trickled in… They'd offered her a three-month contract to go on the reality TV show. She was being tutored on set, so she wasn't coming back to school this year.

"I feel sorry for the tutor," Terence said.

Interestingly, this made more people than just me happy. Even the teachers seemed happier. Mr Little cleaned up his classroom and spent less time looking at his clipboard. And I didn't get another mean text message after that either.

This was the first part of Huia's plan. She said she knew getting rid of Serena would make me happy, but she was surprised by how it had made the rest of the school happy, too.

The weather was good too. The eternal rain had stopped, and it was sunny and getting warmer every day. There were still clouds in the sky, but they were the white fluffy version, not the low hanging grey ones. A buzz of cicadas started filling the air and the clocks were switched back for what here they called 'Daylight saving' so the evenings were long and light.

Huia then told me her second condition: that we explored Auckland some more and so that was what we'd been doing.

Every Saturday we'd choose an adventure. Sometimes we took Terence, sometimes we took Stevie, even Mum came with me once or twice, although I almost banned her after the first trip because she kept asking Huia too many questions about her periods. Huia said she didn't mind, but it *was* a bit weird.

So far, we'd been up Maungawhau again, to Cornwall Park/ Maungakiekie, we'd taken a ferry to Devonport, had ice-creams on the beach and explored the second-hand bookshops. We'd been thrifting (or op-shopping, as they called it) on Karangahape Road, where all the cool alternative people went ("See Maggie, Auckland is cool too," said Huia). We'd walked down Ponsonby Road and goggled at how expensive all the designer clothes were. We'd been to the zoo, and the museum and the Museum of Transport and Technology (that was a bit stupid, but of course Stevie LOVED it). We went to Mission Bay and lay on the beach, and to Kelly Tarlton's aquarium and blew kisses to the sting rays.

I really had gotten it wrong, there was so much to do in Auckland, I had just not been looking for it. We'd even made plans to do a short overnight tramp (what they call hiking here). I sure was turning into a real Kiwi.

The final condition that Huia had put on me when I was negotiating to be friends again was going to happen tonight. I was a bit nervous, but luckily Mum had agreed to come along too.

The sun was still high in the sky even though we'd had dinner. Stevie was happily ensconced playing computer games with our next-door neighbour's son. We got into the car and headed back

---

1 **cicada** insect that lives in hot countries and makes a continuous sound in the daytime – 17 **to goggle** to look in surprise – 21 **sting ray** a large flat fish with sharp points on its back – 27 **to negotiate** to discuss sth in order to reach an agreement – 30 **ensconced** settled comfortably

to the school. We pulled into the carpark. The white building was looking as imposing as ever but I didn't think it looked cold, or scary. We didn't go into the white building though, we turned right and walked over to the school marae to join the group of people who were waiting out the front.

There were about thirty to forty people waiting outside, a mixture of ages and nationalities. A couple of faces I recognised, there was Alice, an old friend of Serena's. I asked if there was any more news from Serena.

"She can't tell me if she's won or not – sworn to secrecy, and the show comes out next week. But it sounds like there are modelling agencies interested in her, so I think she's going to have a busy summer."

I nodded. That was good news. I felt warmer to Serena not having had to see her for the last eight weeks.

The group of people in front of the marae suddenly stopped talking and straightened up and the karanga (call) started. It still made my skin tingle. Then a brief welcome speech was made. The group at the front sang a waiata, then we sang one too. I knew enough now to know that it wasn't the done thing to just lip sync, so I'd learnt the waiata 'Te Aroha' with Mum before we came.

I didn't even have to read it off my phone.

Te aroha
Te whakapono
Me te rangimārie.
Tātou, tātou e.

(Love,
Hope,
Peace,
For us all.)

---

10 **to be sworn to secrecy** not allowed to say anything about a certain matter – 18 **to tingle** to have a feeling of excitement on the skin

We were welcomed onto the marae. This time I knew to take off my shoes.

Inside, to my surprise, was Joseph. He looked surprised to see me, but not unhappy. I couldn't really read his face, but his eyes still crinkled up at the edges.

"Kia ora Maggie," he said smiling.

"Kia ora," I said awkwardly, "um … Joseph this is my mum, Louise."

"I didn't think you'd be interested in learning Te Reo," he said.

"Oh, I'm not … Well, I *am* but … ah, it's a long story …," I was a bit flustered.

The Kaiako (teacher) standing at the front of the room cleared his throat.

"Ok, you'd better explain it later," said Joseph, "Let's sit."

We sat down on the cushions on the floor. The marae was beautiful, the same shape as the one up north, with red, white, and black carvings on the walls and a tall high ceiling with a length of wood like a spine down the middle.

The kaiako (teacher) talked first in Te Reo Māori and then said in English, "Welcome, it's so wonderful to see you all, Pākehā, Māori, Tauiwi here, honouring the treaty and learning about our language. It makes us feel honoured that you are here, and our language isn't dying out,'" he used his hand to draw quote marks, "as we've been told for so many years that it would."

"This is the order of what happens in Te Reo Māori class. Every class we'll meet here and have a kōrero (conversation), then we'll split into our three groups – beginners, intermediate and advanced. But before we do that, we'll have a kaputī – a cup of tea and a biscuit. Before you nourish the mind, you must nourish the stomach!"

---

11 **flustered** embarrassed, confused – 12 **to clear your throat** to make a noise in your throat in preparation to speak – 23 **to die out** to stop existing, disappear – 30 **to nourish** to give necessary food to

People started standing up and moving to the wharekai (eating house).

"Which class are you in, Joseph?" Mum asked.

"I'm in the advanced class – I do speak Te Reo at home but, you know, we've lost some."

"Hey, Joseph," the kaiako (teacher) called over to us.

"Can you pop down to the supermarket on the corner and grab us some milk please? We have run out."

"Want to walk Maggie?" asked Joseph.

"Uh, sure," I said. We headed outside together.

"How long have you been doing classes?" I asked.

"I started when I got down here. It made me feel less lonely – you know, like I was connected to my family."

"Did Serena enjoy it too?"

He looked at me and laughed. "Come on Maggie," he said.

"Did Serena look like the sort of person you think would join a Te Reo class?"

I nodded and laughed.

"How is she, anyway?" I asked, feeling brave.

"Honestly," he said, "I don't know. She broke it off with me as soon as she started on NZ's Next Catwalk Queen."

I was quiet.

"Did you mind?"

"Not really. I mean, I did a little bit, because… well, you know she was really good-looking… but she wasn't genuinely nice, or all that fun to hang out with anyway. And…"

He looked at me and swallowed. "Also, I met someone else, who I started liking."

We were halfway down the road. I could see the supermarket on the corner.

"Oh my god, Joseph, we forgot to put our shoes on."

---

20 **to break it off** to stop a relationship with sb

He laughed and his eyes did that crinkly thing again. "Shoes? You don't need shoes, Maggie! This is New Zealand!"

He walked into the supermarket; bare feet and all.

I stopped and looked down at my feet. I thought, *"Well … when in Rome, …"*

I took a deep breath and followed the cute guy who might be interested in me inside the shop.

The end

What did Maggie realise after she fulfilled Huia's second condition of exploring Auckland more?

Can you complete the saying: 'When in Rome, …'? What does it mean?

Think about it…

Which aspect of language learning do you enjoy the most and why?

Is it important to keep minority languages alive? For what reason?

Activities

Focus on the story

1. Are the sentences True or False?
Tick the correct box.

		True	False
1.	Maggie's mother was unemployed.	☐	☒
2.	Maggie was quite used to flying.	☒	☐
3.	Stevie and Maggie would be going to separate schools.	☒	☐
4.	Some of the volcanoes in Auckland were likely to erupt again soon.	☐	☒
5.	Maggie found it difficult to choose what to wear to school.	☐	☒
6.	Joseph was in the same class as Maggie.	☐	☒
7.	Terence and Huia were studying History at school.	☒	☐
8.	Joseph had only recently taken up rugby.	☐	☒
9.	Maggie had a problem with the food served at the campsite at Waitangi.	☒	☐
10.	The marae that they visited in Waitangi had plain beige walls.	☐	☒
11.	When Maggie's mother took them away for the weekend. Maggie knew what she was planning.	☐	☒
12.	Stevie was trying to keep the water hole on the beach filled up with hot water.	☐	☒
13.	When the accident happened to Stevie, the lifeguards reacted fast.	☒	☐
14.	Maggie's mum went with Stevie in the ambulance to hospital.	☐	☒
15.	Stevie lost his appetite in the hospital because he was feeling ill.	☐	☒

16. Terence told Maggie that she should spend more time learning about New Zealand and its traditions. ☒ ☐
17. Huia enjoyed trying to fix other people's problems. ☒ ☐
18. The teacher, Mr Little, recognised Kevin from the reality TV show immediately. ☐ ☒
19. Serena felt she didn't deserve to take part in the reality show. ☐ ☒
20. Maggie managed to learn a song off by heart for her final visit to the marae. ☒ ☐

2. What happened when?

Put the events in the correct order. Write the number in the correct box below.

a	Maggie forgets to take her shoes off.	5
b	Stevie almost drowns.	8
c	Maggie suffers from travel sickness.	4
d	Maggie's mum makes an important decision.	1
e	Maggie's friend Huia stops talking to her.	6
f	Serena is chosen for a reality show.	10
g	Maggie watches Joseph play rugby.	2
h	Maggie decides to make a fresh start and try harder.	9
i	Maggie and her mum focus on an important conversation on the beach.	7
j	Maggie is bullied by Serena over Joseph.	3

3. What did they look like?

Match the descriptions to the places in the story.

1 rainy, green, small houses (f)	a Maggie's new school
2 cold, empty, boring colour scheme	b the beach with the hot springs (3)
3 people jogging or walking uphill (b)	c their new house in NZ
4 large cold white building	d the campsite in Waitangi
5 H-shaped goalposts	e the scene outside the airport
6 soft blankets, colourful walls	f the holiday apartment (1)
7 white sand and surfers	g the school field
8 picnic tables and a large cooking pit	h Mt Eden, Auckland

4. What happened here?

Write a brief description of something that happened in each place.

1 Maggie's new school

the Maggie school it war good she has
friend Huia and serena hadt serena.

2 the beach with the hot springs

Stevie filld the hauld coult water

3 the campsite in Waitangi

Maggie forget her shose in the Mare

4 the school field

Maggie Fagt with Serena beause Maggie and
Joseph

5 the supermarket in Mt Eden, Auckland

Focus on the people

1. What were they like?

Match the character from the story with some of their main characteristics.

| a Maggie   b Maggie's mum   c Serena   d Stevie   e Mr Little |

1 <u>Maggie's mum</u> liked to be the centre of attention.
2 <u>Mr. Little</u> always made notes and lists of things to do.
3 <u>Mr. Little</u> spent a lot of time trying to stay positive.
4 <u>Maggie</u> didn't make much effort to fit in.
5 <u>Serena</u> didn't seem to be aware of much outside school.
6 <u>Stevie</u> was continually hungry.
7 <u>Maggie</u> was interested in the effect of hormonal changes on the body.
8 <u>Serena</u> made people generally feel upset or unhappy.
9 <u>Maggie</u> had difficulty in overcoming feelings of nostalgia.
10 <u>Maggie's mum</u> enjoyed being helpful to others.

2. Joseph – character assessment.

In the story, Joseph showed many interesting sides of his personality. Find five qualities he showed and give an example of each from the story.

Joseph	
His qualities	Examples

Focus on grammar

1. Mixed past tenses

Choose the correct form of the verb to complete the sentences.

1 Maggie has often been abroad. Her visit to New Zealand was not the first time she **had flown / was flying**.

2 Her grandparents live in France and she and Stevie **have / used** to visit them there.

3 Maggie was not impressed by the NZ scenery. When they arrived, it **rained / was raining** and not very warm at all.

4 Terence and Huia were shocked to hear that Maggie **was having / had** little knowledge of rugby.

5 At school, Maggie **didn't / hadn't** find it easy to find vegetarian dishes.

6 In the classroom, Maggie felt uncomfortable that Serena **would / had** stare at her all the time.

7 At the Waitangi marae, Maggie felt a bit embarrassed that she **wasn't / hadn't** been studying her history.

8 While Maggie, her mum and Stevie **were heading / used to head** for the beach and the weather was bad, she didn't understand. What was going on?

9 It might be said that if Stevie hadn't had his accident, Maggie **didn't / wouldn't** have come to her senses and started to try and be a little bit more like him.

10 Maggie didn't know that Huia **has / had** organised for Kevin to come to the school and take Serena away to go on the show.

2. The active and passive rules

Write active or passive in the correct box to complete the rules about when to use them.

a	• when sb else does the action or when the person doing the action is unknown • uses the verb *to be* in the correct tense plus the past participle of the verb	
b	• when the person or thing mentioned does the action • uses the verb in the correct tense according to the time frame that is being used	

3. Choose the active or passive form to complete the sentences. Use a suitable tense.

1 Maggie and her family _____ (take) to their new home by a taxi from the airport.

2 Maggie _____ (watch) the rugby match that Joseph was playing in.

3 Maggie _____ (send) an anonymous text message – but she suspected it was from Serena.

4 Maggie _____ (forget) to tell her teacher that she didn't eat meat.

Build your vocabulary

Focus on words

1. Which word fits best?

Choose the correct word a, b or c.

1 My little brother's only two and he has _____ every day! When will he grow up?

a threats b screams c tantrums

2 Sometimes they say that a little bit of internal _____ is needed to understand yourself better.

a reflection b realisation c negotiation

3 Have you _____ your doctor? I think it would be a good idea to get a second opinion.

a offended b assessed c consulted

4 The teacher _____ when she saw the state of Mac's homework – it was covered in scribbles!

a clenched b frowned c mocked

5 Proof of identity is _____ in order to take part in public examinations.

a permanent b apparent c mandatory

6 In their _____ , the boys said they were unaware that it was illegal to ride their bikes in the park.

a condition b defence c mishap

2. Word formation

Complete the sentences with the correct form of the word in brackets. You will have to add something onto the end and/or the beginning of the word.

1 We had a very _____ holiday last summer – my father hit his head on a rock in the sea and ended up in hospital! (EVENT)

2 'Did you forget to brush your hair this morning, Sal?' my sister said _____ . (SARCASTIC)

3 All I wanted to do after the argument was to go away and listen to some _____ music. (SOOTHE)

4 Leaving rubbish lying around is _____ for everyone. Please use the bins provided! (HYGIENE)

5 The castle on top of the hill was the most _____ structure for miles around. (IMPOSE)

6 Matt was so annoying on the school trip – he spent his time _____ (SNIGGER) with his pals at the back of the coach.

New in New Zealand – the mind map

You can add any words from the glossary to this mind map for your own learning.

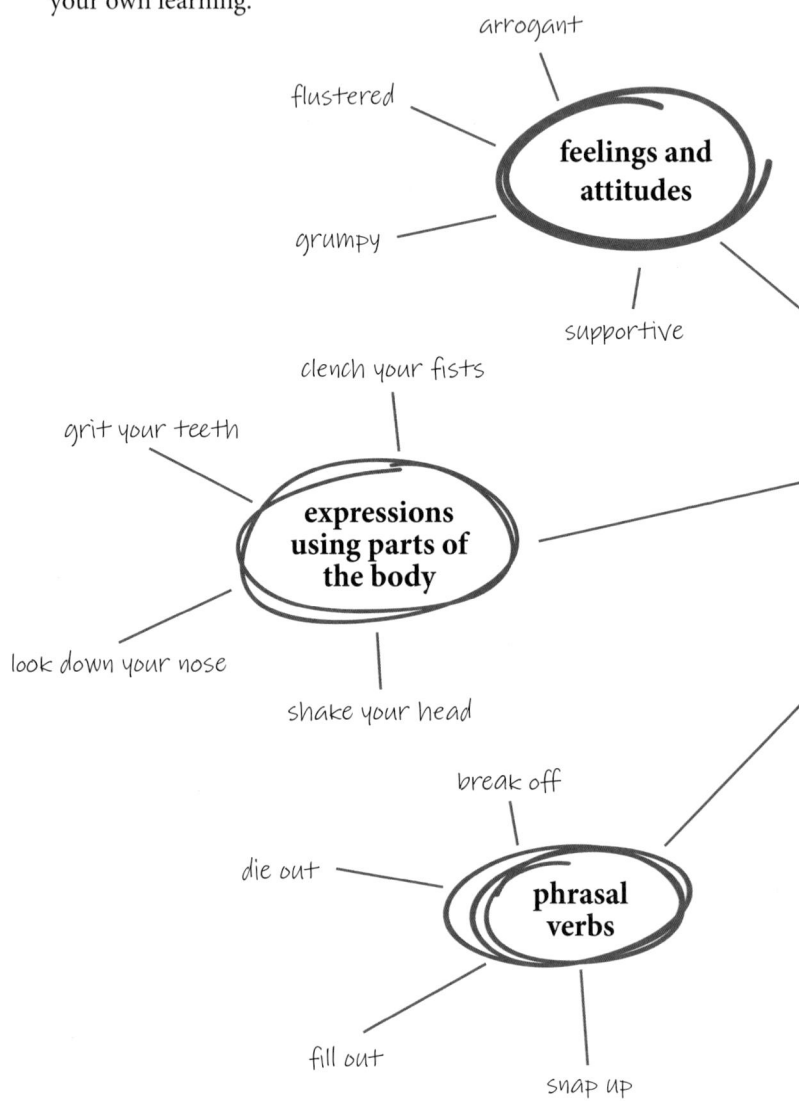

arrogant

flustered

feelings and attitudes

grumpy

supportive

clench your fists

grit your teeth

expressions using parts of the body

look down your nose

shake your head

break off

die out

phrasal verbs

fill out

snap up

whinge

mutter

verbs to do with
speaking / making
noises

mumble

complain

New in
New Zealand

race

actions

jog

drag

crouch

mountain

extinct

nature and
landscape

tide

crater

lush

Glossary

New word?   **Notes / connected words**

Feelings and attitudes

apprehensive   ☐
arrogant   ☐
bemused   ☐
concerned   ☐
flustered   ☐
grumpy   ☐
offensive   ☐
overwhelming   ☐
self-absorbed   ☐
supportive   ☐

Expressions using parts of the body

clear your throat   ☐
clench your fists   ☐
grit your teeth   ☐
look down your nose   ☐
roll your eyes   ☐
send shivers up your spine   ☐
shake your head   ☐
shrug your shoulders   ☐

Phrasal verbs

break off   ☐
die out   ☐
fan out   ☐
fill out   ☐
fill up   ☐
fit in   ☐
mill around   ☐
pull up   ☐

	New word?	Notes / connected words
snap up	☐	
throw up	☐	
trail off	☐	
whisk away	☐	

Verbs to do with speaking / making noises

	New word?
groan	☐
mumble	☐
mutter	☐
shriek	☐
snigger	☐
wail	☐
whinge	☐

Nature and landscape

	New word?
cicada	☐
crater	☐
dormant	☐
extinct	☐
fence	☐
haystack	☐
lawn	☐
lush	☐
raindrop	☐
sting ray	☐
tide	☐
volcano	☐

Actions

	New word?
crouch	☐
drag	☐

	New word?	Notes / connected words
lug	☐	
poke	☐	
pounce	☐	
slam	☐	
squash	☐	
stalk off	☐	
stomp off	☐	
tackle	☐	
twitch	☐	
wade	☐	

Find out more

Find out more

1. The Māori people are New Zealand's indigenous people. Find out five interesting facts about them.

1	
2	
3	
4	
5	

2. Now compare the Māori culture and way of life to yours. Write down some similarities and differences.

Similarities	Differences

3. Write down some important words in your language that you
would use to talk to a foreigner about your culture. Find out
the meaning of the words you have written in English.

My culture	
Words in my language	Words in English
- Aroha	- love
- Awa	- river or valley
- haere mai	- welcome
- Haka	- dance
- Ahi	- Fire
- Ao	- cloud
- Aotearoa	- New zealand
- Ara	- path or road
- Hau	- wind
- Hui	- meeting
- Ika	- fish
- Iti	- small
- Kai	- Food
- Kia ora	- Hi, hello

Answer key

Focus on the story
Questions at the end of each chapter
Chapter 1
- She uses the Queen, the Beatles, tea and castles.
- Sometimes we say sth too confidently which is later proved wrong.

Chapter 2
- It had been raining at the airport, and outside their house it was grey and cold.
- Everyone seemed to be out taking some form of exercise, running, walking, biking etc.

Chapter 3
- Yes, he was, and we know that because he used a friendly tone of voice, and also expressed solidarity with Maggie when he said he knew what it was like to be new at the school.
- Yes, it changed slightly because he was put in a difficult situation when Maggie complained to Serena about the school and Serena got offended. Joseph had to support Serena since she was his girlfriend.

Chapter 4
- Maggie feels that there wouldn't be such strong support for a particular sport from schoolchildren in London.
- Because Serena suspects there is an attraction between Maggie and Joseph.

Chapter 5
- Because she hadn't done her History homework.
- The fact that she'd received an anonymous text message.

Chapter 6

- The problem was that there hadn't been clarity in the translation which led to loss of land by the Māori people.
- Maggie was so absorbed in thinking about the text message she'd received that she failed to see other people's shoes at the doorway. She also hadn't done the relevant reading to alert her to the fact that people normally took off their shoes before entering the marae.

Chapter 7

- Because she had a particular plan in mind, that is, to take them to the hot springs.
- Stevie had probably been so absorbed in getting water in his bucket that he hadn't realised the strength of the waves and the current.

Chapter 8

- She collapsed after all the tension of wondering whether Stevie was going to be alright.
- The epiphany was that Maggie finally understood she had to start trying to like it in New Zealand and not complain all the time. In other words, she needed to have an attitude more like that of her brother.

Chapter 9

- Maggie's motto of WWSD meant that she would try to approach Huia rather than simply being annoyed and not trying to improve the situation herself.
- NZ 101 means the basic information a person needs to and should know about life in New Zealand.

Chapter 10

- We understand that Mr Little was not really up-to-date with current popular shows on TV. Neither had he been informed about the arrival of Kevin on the school premises.
- Kevin means that there had been a secret informer at the school who had contacted him about Serena.

Chapter 11

- Maggie realised that there was an awful lot more to do and see there than she had previously been able to appreciate.
- 'When in Rome, do as the Romans do.' This saying means that when you are visiting a different place or country, you should try to adapt to their way of life as much as possible.

Focus on the story

1 1 F, 2 T, 3 T, 4 F, 5 F, 6 F, 7 T, 8 F, 9 T, 10 F, 11 F, 12 F, 13 T, 14 F, 15 F, 16 T, 17 T, 18 F, 19 F, 20 T
2 1 d, 2 g, 3 j, 4 c, 5 a, 6 e, 7 I, 8 b, 9 h, 10 f
3 1 E, 2 C, 3 H, 4 A, 5 G, 6 F, 7 B, 8 D
4 Students' own answers, whatever they remember in particular.

Focus on the people

1 1 c, 2 e, 3 b, 4 a, 5 e, 6 d, 7 b, 8 c, 9 a, 10 d
2 Joseph's qualities and examples:
   Patience: When Maggie didn't know what the words in Māori meant.
   Loyalty: He was loyal to his background and his roots which showed in his keenness to learn the Māori language.
   Kindness: He helped Maggie out in the beginning, when she started school.
   Sporty: He was in the rugby First Fifteen.
   Humility: Despite being good at sports, good-looking and popular, he was not big-headed about it – unlike Serena.

Focus on grammar

1 1 had flown, 2 used to, 3 was raining, 4 had, 5 didn't, 6 would, 7 hadn't, 8 were heading, 9 wouldn't, 10 had
2 a passive, b active
3 1 were taken / had been taken, 2 watched, 3 was sent / had been sent, 4 had forgotten / forgot

Focus on words

1 1 c, 2 a, 3 c, 4 b, 5 c, 6 b
2 1 eventful, 2 sarcastically, 3 soothing, 4 unhygienic,
   5 imposing, 6 sniggering

Find out more

1 (suggested answers)
   They greet each other by pressing foreheads and noses.
   They cook their food in pits in the ground.
   They love telling stories.
   They have their own language.
   Many have special tattoos that identify their families.
   Music and dance form a very important part of their lives.

2 / 3 Students' own answers.